The Toy Store

Y0-BPU-050

Counting

Lisa Greathouse

Consultants

Chandra C. Prough, M.S.Ed.
National Board Certified
Newport-Mesa
  Unified School District

Jodene Smith, M.A.
ABC Unified School District

Publishing Credits

Dona Herweck Rice, *Editor-in-Chief*
Lee Aucoin, *Creative Director*
Chris McIntyre, M.A.Ed., *Editorial Director*
James Anderson, M.S.Ed., *Editor*
Aubrie Nielsen, M.S.Ed., *Associate Education Editor*
Neri Garcia, *Senior Designer*
Stephanie Reid, *Photo Editor*
Rachelle Cracchiolo, M.S.Ed., *Publisher*

Image Credits

Cover Photolibrary.com; p.12 Stanko07/Dreamstime; p.14 Edith Layland/Dreamstime; p.19 Stuartbur/iStockphoto; p.20 jonnysek/Bigstock; All other images: Shutterstock

Teacher Created Materials

5301 Oceanus Drive
Huntington Beach, CA 92649-1030
http://www.tcmpub.com
ISBN 978-1-4333-3429-0
© 2012 Teacher Created Materials, Inc.
Printed in China
Nordica.092018.CA21801160

Table of Contents

1 one

I count the toys!
I count **1** toy truck.

2 two

I count **2** balls.

3 three

I count **3** bears.

4 four

I count 4 wagons.

5 five

I count 5 robots.

6 six

I count **6** ducks.

7 seven

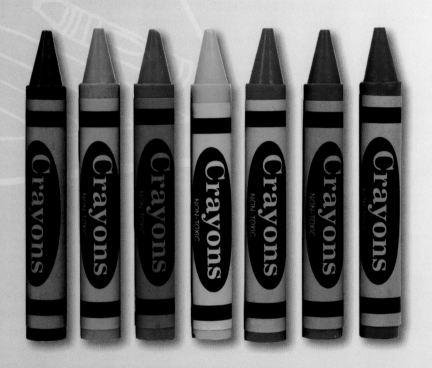

I count **7** crayons.

8 eight

I count **8** kites.

9 nine

I count 9 horses.

10 ten

I count **10** dinosaurs.

11 eleven

I count **11** pails.

12 twelve

I count **12** planes.

13 thirteen

I count **13** bikes.

14 fourteen

I count **14** cars.

15 fifteen

I count **15** drums.

16 sixteen

I count **16** trains.

17 seventeen

I count **17** boats.

18 eighteen

I count **18** bugs.

19 nineteen

I count **19** marbles.

20 twenty

I count **20** blocks.

Count the balls.
Which group has 8 balls?

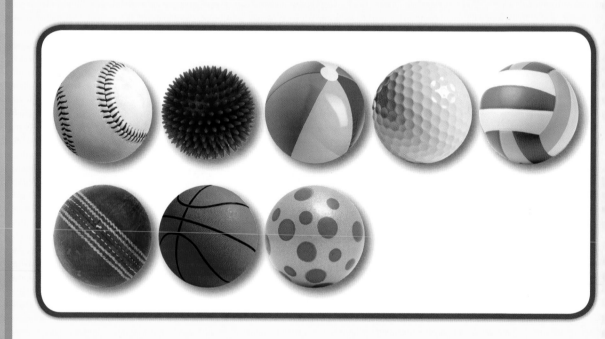

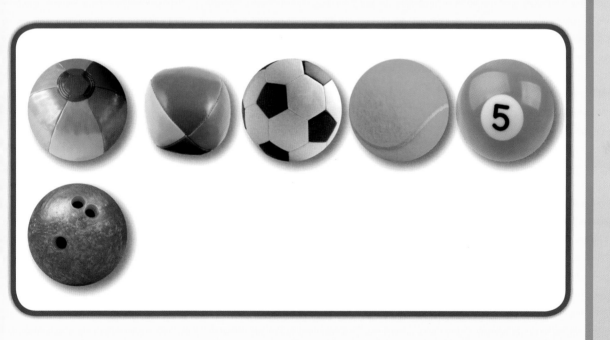

Count the toys.

Which group has 12 toys?

SOLVE THE PROBLEM

How many blocks can you hold?

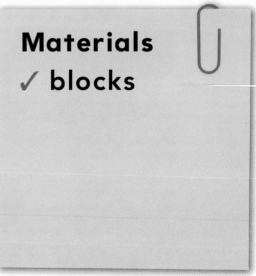

Materials

✓ blocks

1 Get 2 handfuls of blocks.

2 Stack the blocks.

3 Count the blocks out loud.

Glossary

1	one	•
2	two	••
3	three	•••
4	four	••••
5	five	•••••
6	six	••••••
7	seven	•••••••
8	eight	••••••••
9	nine	•••••••••
10	ten	••••••••••

11	eleven	
12	twelve	
13	thirteen	
14	fourteen	
15	fifteen	
16	sixteen	
17	seventeen	
18	eighteen	
19	nineteen	
20	twenty	

You Try It!

Pages 24–25:
The group on the left has eight (8) balls.

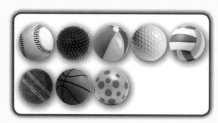

Pages 26–27:
The group on the right has twelve (12) toys.

Solve the Problem

Answers will vary.